MAYBE
Lenormand

FORTUNE TELLING GUIDEBOOK

———•◆•———

By Ryan Edward

PUBLISHED BY U.S. GAMES SYSTEMS, INC. ◆ STAMFORD, CT USA

Copyright © 2016 U.S. Games Systems, Inc.

All rights reserved. All illustrations, design, and content are protected by copyright. No part of this booklet may be reproduced in any form without permission in writing from the publisher, except by a reviewer who wishes to quote brief passages in connection with a review written for inclusion in a magazine, newspaper or website.

10 9 8 7 6 5 4

Made in China

– *For Camelia* –

U.S. GAMES SYSTEMS, INC.
179 Ludlow Street · Stamford, CT 06902 USA
www.usgamesinc.com

INTRODUCTION

The Petit Lenormand is a 19th century 36-card oracle deck borrowing from German cartomancy as well as tea leaf and coffee ground symbol reading. Many prefer it over Tarot and other oracle card systems for its practical and literal sense of the world around any person. The Grand Tableau can give an overview of your well-being, or a detailed answer to a specific situation. Its readings are that of relationships; left right above or below, where cards intersect or disperse, where they meet near or far, if they are surrounded by negative or positive cards. The Lenormand is a pack of cards relying on elegance and particularity. The cards have a narrower focus, and are read in an almost grammatical structure. While you could say reading Tarot cards is like reading panels of a comic book to tell a story, the Lenormand is like a string of Emoji to spell out a specific message.

Maybe Lenormand works to honor that Lenormand tradition. Its illustrations are designed to convey the meaning, folklore, and heart of each card's personality. While in most every way it follows the pattern of Lenormand from over a hundred years ago, it does have one major difference. This deck has 52 cards, rather than 36. Cards 37-52 borrow from a tangent lineage of fortune telling decks to complete the common 52-card playing card pack, merging several divination traditions.

You can use the first 36 cards of this pack as any other traditional Lenormand. However, using the added cards, you are playing with something else, the Maybe Lenormand.

If you are new to Lenormand, work with the original 36 cards to get a sense of how they read. Once you are comfortable, add the rest of the pack. Enjoy!

READING THE CARDS

As always when reading, the question and context are vitally important to how you interpret the cards. Once you have decided on a precise question, focus with intent, and shuffle until you are ready to lay out the cards in a pre-designated arrangement.

The Lenormand cards are read in a specific order; reading the card to the right to modify or clarify the card to its left. For example, we have the Letter for the first card. This could be a message or note. If the card to its right is the Heart, we have a love letter. If it's near the Birds card, the communication may be via Twitter or instant chatting. With the Thundercloud, the meaning is very bad news. With the Clover, it could be a short joke. Cards are rarely read alone; they are more useful in groupings of two or more. Look to the card above to see its intentions. See what cards are near or far. Determine where cards' lines cross and meet.

THE GRAND TABLEAU

While the Lenormand can often be read in smaller lines, the original and fundamental layout uses all 36 cards. Many readers like to work up to learning the Grand Tableau (GT), but if you are reading the relationships at play, the GT can be easier to dissect than a five-card string. When you lay all 36 cards, you'll always have your subject in sight, so you can see where it crosses with concerns of love, money, work, or anything else defined by another card. Simply because it uses many cards does not mean the answer is verbose; often it is still very sharp and to the point.

- SAMPLE GRAND TABLEAU READING -

04 · 01 · 27 · 36 · 22 · 13 · 34 · 17

16 · 06 · 05 · 02 · 24 · 03 · (29) · 25

21 · 19 · 15 · 23 · 33 · 26 · 10 · 12

18 · 14 · 32 · 09 · 30 · 07 · 11 · 35

08 · 31 · (28) · 20

A female querent is interested to see if she will have a love interest soon. From this spread, we can tell this

Lady (29) has a positive relationship in her near future, as the Ring (25) falls directly to her right. We draw lines from the Lady and the Gentleman (28) to see where they meet at the Heart (24). Card 24 is flanked by the Clover (2) and the Ship (3), a good time and fun adventure awaits with this love interest. We look to the cards around 28 to see more about him. He is flanked by the Sun (31) and Park (20), indicating that he is rather popular and seen by many. The Lily (30) rests above him, a sign of virtue. Things bode very well for our Lady's interests.

When you avoid reading the Grand Tableau as a set spread and open yourself to how the cards relate to each other and interact, the elegance of the Lenormand is heard loud and clear.

THREE-CARD STRINGS

Lenormand cards are very rarely read with fewer than three cards. A three-card reading should give you a short, simple answer with a subject, modifier, and some action or outcome. A few examples are given on the following pages.

— EXAMPLE 1 —

A Gentleman wonders if he'll win a court case.

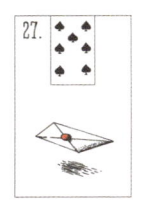

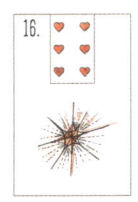

Bring documentation (Ring + Letter) and you'll get your wish (Star).

— EXAMPLE 2 —

A querent lost her wallet, where is it?

In her backpack (Book + Rider) in the back yard (Park).

— EXAMPLE 3 —

Will there be a second date?

Not anytime soon. A clouded heart leads to boredom (Trees).

— EXAMPLE 4 —

How should I plan my project?

Go through multiple rounds of edits (Scythe + Birch Rod) before showing for a group review (Birch Rod + Park).

— EXAMPLE 5 —

I'm going out tonight with friends.
What should I expect?

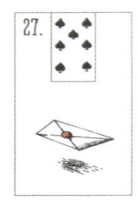

Travel certainly (Ship + Rider), perhaps across a river where you'll meet a gentleman. You'll text with him (Rider + Letter) later into the night.

FIVE-CARD DAILY LINE

Some people use three-cards for a daily morning reading. Lenormand is very mundane in this regard and often points to a specific moment or event. Without knowing if this is during your workday, at school or in the evening, it can be hard to decipher. For this reason I like to use five cards to help establish a time frame.

CARDS 1-3 speak to the day, if it's your day job, school, or personal time.

| 1 | 2 | 3 | 4 | 5 |

CARDS 3-5 speak to your evening, when you get home from work, or start your night job.

THE CENTER CARD (3) speaks to the tone of the day, and the transition from day to night. If you work 9-5 and wonder if you will have to work late, look to card 3. If it's the Mountain, sorry, you're stuck at work. If it's the Child or the Rider, be free! Enjoy your evening. The center card carries or blocks your flow from day into evening.

— EXAMPLE 1 —

A woman with a 9 to 5 job.

This busy Woman has many meetings (Park) throughout today. After she finishes some e-mails or written communication, she'll be able to leave work and focus on her commitment (Ring) to her child. She may have made a promise via text message (Letter – Ring) to see the child.

— EXAMPLE 2 —

A male college student.

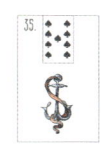

Our querent will spend the morning at home (or dorm maybe in this case) before a best friend (Dog + Anchor) comes to visit (House + Dog). Later on, he'll be stuck at work (Anchor) with a woman, but will have a joyful evening with her (Lady + Sun).

CARD MEANINGS
1 to 36

Following are descriptions for the 36 basic cards. This is how I best understand them and how they function, interact, and influence the cards around them. Each card is much more than a set of fixed meanings, but has its own unique quality. Understanding these qualities intimately and how they mix and relate to one another is the key to reading the Lenormand.

Each card is given a title. Think of it as its core; all nuances and meanings are derived from this single word. Following it, a few sentences give a general overview describing the card's symbolism. Next are some characteristics on how this card may represent or describe a person. The 'querent' is the person for whom or about whom the reading is being done. The term 'significator' refers to the card that represents that person. Lastly, there is a short list of five or six keywords, given in order of importance.

- CARD 1 -
RIDER: ARRIVAL

News travels fast. The Rider comes to you as a person, a message, or a delivery. From afar, he comes from some distance and removed from you, he is possibly a stranger. If he is near to the significator, the arrival comes sooner, and is more personal.

The Rider is swift, moving from point A to point B at a moment's notice. As a person, he may come in and out of your life. For a female querent, he may become a fling. For a gay male querent, this is his lover, actual or prospective. Regardless of sexuality, he is tall, lean, fit, ambitious and well-dressed.

KEYWORDS: News, Visitor, Swiftness, Luggage, Well-dressed, Vehicle

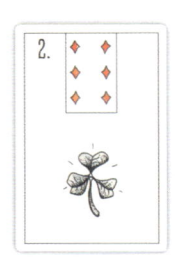

-CARD 2-
CLOVER: FUN

To quote Shakespeare, "Brevity is the soul of wit." The Clover is a snap of the fingers, a flash in the pan. It is a bit of luck on a good day, a fleeting thought to catch, or a little extra cash in hand. Close to the significator, fortune looks well, but removed or clouded, misfortune awaits.

The Clover card signifies a person with a sharp sense of humor and wit. He may be the class clown or the prankster. He could have green or hazel eyes, maybe even of Irish descent. Sexually, this may be a quick romp.

KEYWORDS: Luck, Wit, Brief, Green, Small, Cash

- CARD 3 -
SHIP: DISTANCE

The ship travels. It could signify a vacation if close to the significator. As a business, it is prosperous, potentially a global endeavor. Describing a love, there is a deep longing for someone, possibly due to distance.

The Ship may signify a person who is foreign to the querent's location. Physically, this card describes someone with olive skin. They also may be successful in business, trade or stocks.

KEYWORDS: Travel, Distance, Trade, Foreign, Water, Longing

- CARD 4 -
HOME: PERSONAL

The home is both your hat and where you hang it. It is everything close to you—your family and your personal belongings. It is the people living with you, whether your family, roommates, or those in your dormitory. If this card is near the center and underneath the significator, guard your domain.

This is the first court card in the deck, the King of Hearts. Describing a person, he is a family man, likely the father of the querent. Physically, he may be of stocky stature.

KEYWORDS: Home, Family, Father, Square, Blocky, Personal Endeavors

- CARD 5 -
TREES: LIFE

Trees grow, some for thousands of years, gaining wisdom and experience. This is the mind, body and spirit of the querent. While the House can be your immediate family, the Trees can be your extended cousins and such, the family tree. Near the querent, especially above the significator, beware of health concerns. From a distance and surrounded by other positive cards, vigor and vitality ensues.

As a person, this is a healer, a shaman, or one in touch with nature. Otherwise, this could mean a person who might be a bit boring and slow to tell a story.

KEYWORDS: Health, Nature, Time, Slow, Boring, Spirit

-CARD 6-
THUNDERCLOUD: TURBULENCE

Clouds rolls in and darkness follows. This card forebodes misfortune for all surrounding cards. If far, things are more pleasant. When things are cloudy, we cannot see. Confusion surrounds this card. A bit of a silver lining is to the left corner; you may find a sliver of positivity there.

The King of Clubs is a shady figure. He uses his wife, the Serpent, to twist the truth, and his son, the Birch Rod, to instigate an argument on his behalf. Beware this man on all fronts. Speaking strictly physically, this may indicate a person with gray or two-toned hair.

KEYWORDS: Gloom, Opaque, Weather, Smoke, Confusion, Dark/Gray

- CARD 7 -
SERPENT: TROUBLE

Many believe the first lie was told by a serpent. As it bends the truth, things become complicated. Betrayal, blame, and jealousy follow. Don't trip over its deceit.

As a woman, she can be unlikable, above 40, and wears glasses. Noted as "the other woman," she may be the one with whom the Gentleman has an affair, or the partner for a lesbian querent.

KEYWORDS: Treachery, Other Woman, Complication, Rivers, Cords, Sharp-tongued

- CARD 8 -
COFFIN: WITHOUT

Illness and loss of fortune await, especially if close by. From afar, be cautious of its surrounding cards. Things end here, but not suddenly; they wither and rot. Things don't become transformed with the coffin. They just die.

Physically, this person may have dark or sharp features. Personally, they may be depressing, dark or simply macabre. It also describes things underground or in a box.

KEYWORDS: Death, Grim, Loss, Illness, Debt, Box

- CARD 9 -
BOUQUET: DELIGHT

Near or far, pleasantries surround this card. It could be a surprise, a gift, an invitation, or something beautiful, but it's likely to put a smile on your face.

The Queen of Spades is a friendly woman. She could have blond hair and be quite beautiful, with a rather upbeat disposition.

KEYWORDS: Surprise, Gift, Pretty, Creative, Flowers, Charming

- CARD 10 -
SCYTHE: CUT

Beware, the right side points to danger. The blade slices all in its path, be it relationships, contracts, or hope. Surrounded by positive cards, it could bode well for a fall harvest. But in general, peril awaits.

The Jack of Diamonds is opportunistic. He is certainly sharp. He or his Queen can pose for a son- or daughter-in-law respectively. Personally, it may describe a person with a short and curt demeanor.

KEYWORDS: Danger, Slice, Harvest, Edit, Autumn, Abrupt

-CARD 11-
BIRCH ROD: QUARREL

There is discord among others, rifts within the family, and disharmony between spouses. Things go back and forth, but refuse to halt. It creates so much friction it can inflict a fever. Krampus comes to punish. It is both a repetitive action, and a physical motion. The French term *la verge* means both the Birch and the penis.

As a Jack, this person is a brat and can be hard to deal with, argumentative without doubt. Physically, he may exercise regularly, and thus have a great physique.

KEYWORDS: Discord, Repetition, Correction, Friction, Manual, Phallus

- CARD 12 -
BIRDS: AFLUTTER

Flapping about, nearby they cause anxiety and from afar they pose a sudden trip. A little bird divulges many secrets, and two create gossip. Things spread by word of mouth. Conversations surround this card.

Describing a person, they could have a bird-like face, beady eyes and a long nose. Personally, they could be fidgety and nervous. It may be two people, possibly elderly.

KEYWORDS: Unease, Sorrow, Trips, Communication, Gossip, Couples

- CARD 13 -
CHILD: WONDER

Children admire so much of what captures their attention. Easy to make friends, the Child is a card of good associations, support and novelty.

While mostly supportive, this person could be naïve or immature. Physically, young in age or short in stature. It also represents children and grandchildren.

KEYWORDS: Ally, Children, New, Naïve, Small, Young

- CARD 14 -
FOX: SLY

He stalks his prey. If near to you, beware of those around you with ulterior motives. If far, there is no severe threat. He's duplicitous, but not always harmful, unless followed by negative cards. Some may say he represents work, though more like a side gig, or freelance work, your "hustle" if you will.

As a person, they can be manipulative and cunning. Physically, they may have red hair, or be petite and light on their feet.

KEYWORDS: Cunning, Mischievous, Duplicitous, Stalk, Silent, Side Job

- CARD 15 -
BEAR: POSSESS

Bears gain weight for the winter and protect their cubs relentlessly. This is a card of haves and have-nots. The Bear knows to throw its weight around, and is accustomed to getting what it wants. They are easily envious. Whether this card means caring or jealous may depend on surrounding cards.

Father, mother, boss, or pastor, the Bear is a person who has others to watch over and care for. Physically, they can be heavier.

KEYWORDS: Authority, Own, Envy, Oppress, Weight, Eat

- CARD 16 -
STAR: NOTION

Wish upon a star—ideas become reality, whether by scientific formula, design plan, or a psychic hit. The Star represents both science and astrology. The Magi followed a star to Bethlehem, and sailors crossed oceans by charting constellations. Thus, this card represents destinations or networks.

This card describes a person who is a thinker and a dreamer, one who is easily lost in thought.

KEYWORDS: Idea, Wish, Magic, Intelligence, Network, Destination.

- CARD 17 -
STORK: EVOLVE

Moving home, getting a new job, or having a baby, this is a card of significant change, most always for the better. If nearby, it implies physical relocation. If near the Ship, it might mean air travel. If close to the Child, a baby is coming.

As the Queen of Hearts, many see this card as the mother. Storks eat serpents. If the Queen of Hearts follows the Queen of Clubs, the Serpent is no threat. However, if the Serpent follows the stork, vengeance may play out.

KEYWORDS: Change, Relocate, Advance, Fly, Mother

- CARD 18 -
DOG: FIDELITY

Always happy to see you, the Dog is a card of loyalty and close friendship. It offers unwavering support if nearby. If far and cloudy, it shows a fair-weather friend. This card, of course, also represents our pet dogs.

This person is devoted to you and may have large brown eyes and dark, shaggy hair.

KEYWORDS: Loyal, Friend, Dog, Devotion, Sincerity, Adoration

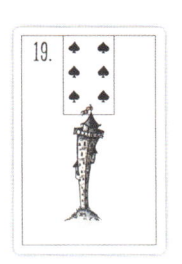

- CARD 19 -
HIGH TOWER: INSTITUTION

So tall it's almost boastful. Towers are modern-day replacements for the Great Pyramids. These looming structures are built to last beyond a lifetime. The High Tower represents all that is larger than any one person: universities, businesses, institutions, and tradition. It is also a card of being secluded and locked away.

If this describes a person, it is someone who thinks very highly of himself. Ego is inherent in this card. We don't build the tallest towers out of modesty. Physically, the person is very tall.

KEYWORDS: Organization, Ego, Solitude, Life Span, Large Buildings

- CARD 20 -
THE PARK: COMMUNAL

Pictured is Art Hill in Forest Park, the crown jewel of Saint Louis. Art Hill is a place where the city gathers for movies, fireworks, or balloon races. At the top is the Art Museum, open to all free of charge. This is a card of the people and the public.

Describing a person, they are very sociable and self-aware. They are put together, like a well-manicured garden, ready to be seen by many people.

KEYWORDS: Gathering, Public, People, Outdoors, Garden, Polished

-CARD 21-
MOUNTAIN: ADVERSARY

This card blocks. Nearby, it is an enemy, from afar it could be a protective friend. The Mountain is great at getting in the way. It is not insurmountable, but difficult to surpass. It's very cold, but the snow is starting to melt.

As a person, they are ornery and persistent. They do not budge. Physically, they may have white hair or be balding.

KEYWORDS: Blockage, Enemy, Obstacle, Stubborn, Cold, Bald

-CARD 22-
WAYS: OPTIONS

North or South, East or West, which way do you go? It is card number twenty-two, two twos. It is a card of opposites and polarity. With a travel card it may represent a journey. Alone, it could be a road.

This person may be of two minds, or indecisive. They may not have a discernible sexuality. As the Queen of Diamonds, this is a sister, step-daughter or an in-law. She could be opportunistic.

KEYWORDS: Choice, Two, Crossroads, Paths, Decide, Roads, Secondary Female

-CARD 23-
MICE: LOSS

The mice take what is yours. This is often intentional, as in theft or robbery. The closer this card is to you, the likelier your chance of recovery. Likewise, it implies pests, be it actual rodents or home-invading insects or company. It may imply a virus or disease, either physical or mental.

As people, you may not want to trust them with your things. They could also be overly anxious, especially with the Birds. Physically, this may imply rat-like facial features, or mousy brown hair.

KEYWORDS: Theft, Pests, Loss, Eat, Disease, Mess

-CARD 24-
HEART: PASSION

The heart holds your inner desire. It pumps your blood and fuels your fervor. Love, happiness and bliss surround this card.

As a person, he can be sensitive and romantic. The Jack of Hearts is an innocent, caring soul. Physically, he may have reddish or heart-shaped features.

KEYWORDS: Love, Desire, Emotion, Sensitive, Red, Blood

- CARD 25 -
RING: BOND

An endless loop, the Ring is an everlasting sign of a commitment. To the right of the significator, this is a successful relationship. But if to the left it means difficulty, broken promises, or divorce are likely. Surrounded by positive cards, there could be some relief. However, with negative cards, unhealthy addiction may follow.

This person is dedicated and possibly in a committed relationship. At worst, they may have bad habits, or obsessive-compulsive disorder. Physically, they have very round features.

KEYWORDS: Relationship, Bond, Promise, Marriage, Addiction, Endless

-CARD 26-
BOOK: KNOWLEDGE

Secrets and learning are contained within the pages of the book. This card refers to things you do not know, or are working to learn. It can be education or training, projects you work on for your job or on the side. The Book is not always accessible, but its information is always valuable. Its importance is indicated by how near it is the person.

This card describes someone who is intelligent, bookish, studious, or very cryptic. With the Moon or Stars, the person may be into mysticism and the occult.

KEYWORDS: Secrets, Project, Lesson, Hidden, Occult, Information

-CARD 27-
LETTER: WORDS

Many words and sentences make up a letter. This is a card of text and news, things written down on paper or on screen. In the 21st century, this includes text messages, email, or even Twitter with the Birds. Beware the Clouds nearby—bad news awaits.

This person may be verbose, or at best have an impressive vocabulary. He or she may be an author, poet, or blogger. This is someone who has a way with words.

KEYWORDS: Written, News, Vocabulary, Eloquent, Text

-CARD 28-
GENTLEMAN: MALE SIGNIFICATOR

If the one being read for is male, this card represents him. All cards laid out are read in relationship to this card, with distance between cards taken into account.

If the querent is female, this card represents a significant man in her life or situation.

- CARD 29 -
LADY: FEMALE SIGNIFICATOR

If the querent is a lady, this card represents her. All surrounding cards are considered in their relationship to her.

If the querent is male, this card signifies an important female in his life or situation.

-CARD 30-
LILY: VIRTUE

Among different cultures, the Lily is a symbol of virginity, virtue, motherhood, fatherhood, or simply sex. This is a card about family, values, and righteousness. Where it occurs gives clue to one's ideals. Above a person, they have good intentions. However, the Lily below a person can signify one with questionable morals.

This person is mature and possibly sexual. As the King of Spades, he is logical, in a scientific or legal field.

KEYWORDS: Moral, Behavior, Well-Mannered, Sex, Reproduction, Paternal

-CARD 31-
SUN: BRIGHT

It is our source of light, joy and life. All is exposed under the sun, happy and warm. Secrets are revealed, lies are confessed, and bad luck turns around in its presence.

The Sun describes those who love the limelight, the center of attention. With the Tower this person may be a megalomaniac, with the Clover a very lucky individual, with the Lily a person with incredible attraction. They may be blond.

KEYWORDS: Joy, Exposure, Luck, Shine, Happiness, Warmth

-CARD 32-
MOON: REFLECTION

The silvery light of the moon enchants us all. If this card falls near the person, it means they are well recognized, and are secure in their reputation. When further away, instability follows as this card indicates notoriety, the questioning of your character and name. Because the Moon card has a strong tie to identity, for many it represents our careers. Today, it may represent all screens, from a TV to a watch face.

The person indicated by this card is well known. With the Tower or Anchor, they may be very career- or ego-driven. With the Star or Book, the person could be described as a bit mystical.

KEYWORDS: Recognition, Honor, Career, Impression, Screens, Fame

-CARD 33-
KEY: ANSWER

Pay attention to where this card lies. A Grand Tableau is a large puzzle, and the Key holds a vital piece of the solution. The key pictured is very simple, which allows it to unlock whatever it needs. The key is standing straight up at attention, an exclamation point to whatever lies beneath.

People described by the Key are physically very lean. Personality wise, they can be very smart (especially with the Book card) or a know-it-all with the Tower. They exude confidence for good or bad.

KEYWORDS: Solution, Highlight, Sure, Reinforce, Unlock

-CARD 34-
FISH: ABUNDANCE

There are plenty of fish in the sea, or so they say. The New Testament recalls Christ feeding 5,000 people with two fish and some bread. Throughout time, the fish has become a symbol of abundance. It represents your affluence. If the card is far, beware of a dry spell.

As a person, the King of Diamonds is all about money. He is good at business and trade, and may enjoy life near water. Physically, the Fish may describe a person with blue eyes.

KEYWORDS: Affluence, Cash, Many, Water, Entrepreneurship, Fish

- CARD 35 -
ANCHOR: GOAL

In the original Game of Hope, this card was Hope, the goal of the game. It is where you want to land. For many it may represent work, what keeps you stable on a day-to-day basis. It is also a symbol of faithfulness and love. The farther this card is from a person, the more unstable they may be.

The Anchor signifies a person who is solid, dependable and goal-oriented. They say what they do and do what they say. Physically, they may have tattoos, and may be a sailor or in the Navy.

KEYWORDS: Hope, Intention, Work, Longing, Stable

-CARD 36-
CROSS: BURDEN

The Cross represents something that is heavy to carry, an albatross. This card may refer to the price we have to pay for our actions. The Cross is a symbol of grief and piety. In the original Game of Hope one of the goals was to not overshoot and land on Card #35, the Cross. If you did, you would fall back a few steps. The Cross is an end. Whatever comes afterwards follows with greater intensity.

As a person, they are troubled. They may play the martyr with the Birch Rod, or seriously have too much going on for any one person. Possibly, they are very religious. The Cross stands for all faiths, not just Christianity.

KEYWORDS: Heavy, Hardship, Onus, Stop, Religion

CARD MEANINGS
37 to 52

These additional 16 cards add a twist to the Lenormand tradition. They are based on a tangential lineage of similar decks, all claiming Mlle Marie Anne Lenormand's ownership. While hardly any of these expanded decks are identical, they carry a very noticeable pattern, even ending on the same card, the Safe.

Since the 36-card 'Petit Lenormand', as it is officially called, is rooted in simplicity, there are those who say extra cards are bothersome. However, with the specificity afforded in the Lenormand cards, there are some very definitive, but different angles one can take on the cards. These extra cards don't 'muddy up' the meanings. Many help carry the secondary focus of other cards in the spread, so once you are using all 52, each card becomes more precise, and thus the readings provide more clarity.

For instance, if I was only using 36 cards, the Flowers could represent 'creativity' as a secondary meaning to 'delight.' However, when using the added cards, the Rose brings the focus to the arts. Now, when I look at Card #9, I know I am focused on 'surprise' because the other angle now rests with Card #40.

-CARD 37-
PIG: OPULENCE

At the feast table for a king, or a 'prize pig' at a state fair, the pig has long been a symbol of success and fulfillment. "High on the hog, hog heaven", and "bringing home the bacon" are all common phrases that equate the Pig to a status of having more than enough.

This person is accustomed to a certain lifestyle. He or she may have very fine taste, only wearing luxury brands, or simply one who likes to eat and stay on the couch.

KEYWORDS: Luxury, Contentment, Wealth, Gain, Success, Relaxed

-CARD 38-
LION: PRIDE

The Lion cares about himself and those close to him. He can be a caring protector ensuring the well-being of those near to him, or a vicious adversary you dare not cross, depending on surrounding cards. Regardless, the Lion rules those around him. From a distance, expect freedom and autonomy from his reign.

As a person, he is about himself first, followed soon by those close to him. This person is not used to being on the sidelines. Physically, he may have a luscious head of hair. This person is prone to an inflated sense of ego.

KEYWORDS: Ruler, Protector, Hair, Predator, Clan, Ego

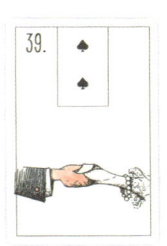

-CARD 39-
HANDS: ACCORD

Two hands meet, likely for the first time. This could be a first encounter with a person, or an agreement with a mate. Compromises are accomplished and deals are stuck. Nearby, this is an encounter with a familiar person. From a distance, you may have never met them before.

This person is good with crowds and working the room. Look to nearby cards to see their intentions.

KEYWORDS: Meet, Agreement, Friendship, Deal, Handshake, Encounter

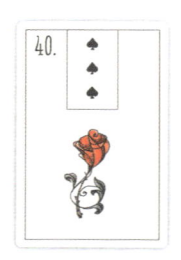

- CARD 40 -
ROSE: ALLURE

The Rose is irresistible. It is an emblem of romance, attraction and beauty. If the Rose appears during a romantic encounter, seduction will likely occur. It is beauty and thus the arts. If next to the Letter, it refers to poetry. It means music when with the Birds card.

This card describes very romantic or artistic people. They can easily entice and attract others. Their work is that of bewitching beauty. Physically, they are rather glamorous or a bit *avant garde.*

KEYWORDS: Charm, Art, Romance, Seduction, Captivate, Tender

-CARD 41-
BACCHUS: REVELRY

Festivities are underway. Break out the wine and let the party begin! This is a card of letting loose with no responsibilities. Be careful if it's surrounded by negative cards, as the drinking could take a turn for the worse.

This describes a partier, or one who at least likes to drink. It could be a frat boy or a *sommelier* depending on context and surrounding cards. Physically, he may be shorter and round.

KEYWORDS: Drinking, Party, Merriment, Levity, Amusement, Plump

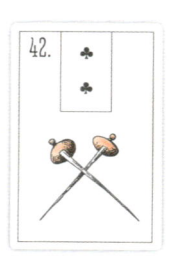

-CARD 42-
RAPIERS: DUEL

En garde! An attack looms. This may be expected from a known rival, or simply a debate opponent. However, this confrontation could pose a harmful surprise. Intensity is indicated by how close this card is to the person.

This person can be harmful with his actions or words. At best, he just likes to disagree and challenge anybody and everybody. When next to the Clover, this card may indicate someone with a "rapier wit." He may also be a person who owns weapons.

KEYWORDS: Attack, Challenge, Debate, Fight, Weapons

-CARD 43-
CATS: SELF-CENTERED

The Cats are what the Dog is not. They denote flattery, but only when it serves them as well.

The Cats card portrays people who are fickle and selfish by nature. You're there to please them, not the other way around. They can be curious to a fault.

KEYWORDS: Flattery, Selfishness, Curious, Fickle, Greedy, Impatient

- CARD 44 -
MEDAL: HONORS

This card is about recognition bestowed, either due to efforts, accomplishment or initiation. Near business and work-related cards, this Medal suggests great success. Next to the Book and Garden, it might mean a secret society.

This person is well-respected and may have been awarded for great duty or service. They are likely members of a group of individuals with very specific common interests.

KEYWORDS: Recognition, Award, Success, Initiation, Club, Order

- CARD 45 -
SICK BED: ILLNESS

Things are not well. Next to a person, this card can indicate actual physical ailment. Next to cards about projects, money and concerns, you should expect failure. The closer to a person, the more severe the threat. However, that is lessened in the presence of Sun and Flame.

This person may be a patient or a caretaker, depending on surrounding cards. With the Fox, they may simply be feigning sickness.

KEYWORDS: Sickness, Malady, Patient, Caretaker, Affliction, Blight

- CARD 46 -
EYE: SIGHT

You could be under watch. Near to the person, this card indicates that close friends are paying attention to you. If far, it signifies suspicion. With the Tower it means 'big brother' is watching. Below you, it indicates that you may be flying above radar.

This person likes to be aware of what's going on; they pay close attention. With the Cats card, he or she may be curiously interested, even a bit nosy. With the Moon or Stars, this person could be a clairvoyant.

KEYWORDS: Watch, Observe, Notice, Attention, Voyeur

- CARD 47 -
FLAME: COMFORT

This is the hearth of the home, a place where everybody gathers. It is an intimate space, one that is safe, warm and bright. It's where our food gets cooked. This could be a campfire with the Trees, a barbecue with the Pig, or watching TV with the Moon. This card lessens the negativity of surrounding cards.

This describes a warm and caring person, one who has a close circle of friends or family. With the Clover or Flowers, this person is rather flamboyant and perhaps has red hair.

KEYWORDS: Warmth, Closeness, Light, Cooking, Fire, Bright

-CARD 48-
CUPID: IMPULSE

Cupid is the lack of will. Whether it is an instant crush, a sexual encounter, or simply your id taking control. When his arrow strikes below, what we know as truth becomes irrelevant. Potency of the arrow is related to distance, so look to surrounding cards to determine its effects.

Those who date often, or who jump from person to person fall under Cupid. They don't always think rationally, and look to intimacy as a crutch. They may have chubby cheeks and curly hair.

KEYWORDS: Crush, Hookup, Capricious, Fickle, Short-term, Baby-faced

-CARD 49-
LIGHTNING: SUDDEN

Like a flash, this card brings the jolt of an unexpected surprise. Look to surrounding cards to see if this is a disaster or a delight. With the Key, an idea has struck. With the Serpent, unexpected peril awaits. Either way, it came from nowhere.

This person can be spontaneous, erratic and unpredictable, with an electric personality. With certain cards, they may be very creative, capturing thoughts and ideas on napkins.

KEYWORDS: Surprise, Shock, Abrupt, Astonish, Electric, Lightning

-CARD 50-
BROKEN MIRROR: SHATTERED

What once was a single, smooth pane of glass is now countless fragments. No good can come from this situation. Split and tossed in all directions, what remains of the mirror reflects a fractured reality; perceptions are smashed. This card's influence is lessened if far, or if surrounded by positive cards.

This may be a person with an unlucky streak. They also may have a fractured sense of reality, especially with themselves. Physically, they're less attractive than anticipated.

KEYWORDS: Disruption, Misperceptions, Bad Luck, Break, Reflections

-CARD 51-
TRAIN: TRAVERSE

While the Ship travels around the globe, the Train moves people and goods across land. It is still a symbol of commerce, but usually domestic as opposed to import and export. The Rider may signify private transport, as in a car, but the Train is public. As an elevated or subway train, it is a lifeblood of cities. We can also vacation via train, but at shorter distances than by ship.

This person is hard to catch. They are speedy and efficient, good with local business and trade. They may live a distance away, but in your region or country.

KEYWORDS: Landlocked Travel, Domestic Business, Public Transportation, Fast, Efficient

-CARD 52-
SAFE: CASH

While the Fish may be your affluence and the Bear your financial stability, the Safe represents your actual funds. The open side of the safe is vulnerable. Positive cards here may hint at incoming cash, but negative cards, especially the Mice or Coffin will deplete it. The closed side is more secure. If this points towards the person, finances should prosper.

This card describes a person tied to money: a stockbroker, an heiress or a bank teller. They are likely great with numbers and the bottom line. They may dress expensively, but not extravagantly.

Keywords: Money, Account, Safe, Financial, Square, Expensive

The
TRÈS GRAND TABLEAU

When reading a tableau with all 52 cards, arrange them with five rows of nine cards with a final row of seven at the bottom. This spread can certainly give you a lot to look at, but don't let it intimidate you. What matters is that you still focus on the relationships between the cards. One added advantage of this larger layout is its 'heart' positions 13-15, 22-24, 31-33, and 41, which gives you a nine-card square to read at its center. You can look here to find the core message or the 'heart of the matter'.

```
01 · 02 · 03 · 04 · 05 · 06 · 07 · 08 · 09
10 · 11 · 12 · 13 · 14 · 15 · 16 · 17 · 18
19 · 20 · 21 · 22 · 23 · 24 · 25 · 26 · 27
28 · 29 · 30 · 31 · 32 · 33 · 34 · 35 · 36
37 · 38 · 39 · 40 · 41 · 42 · 43 · 44 · 45
    46 · 47 · 48 · 49 · 50 · 51 · 52
```

NOTES